DOLLAR COST AVERAGING
&
COVERED CALL STRATEGY

Makes money…

By

Er. SUDHIR KUMAR SAHU

Dedicated to

My parents, my family, my well wishers & my departed brother Dr. Srimanta.

<u>ACKNOWLEDGEMENTS</u>

The support & encouragement of family, friends & well wishers is absolutely necessary to achieve something in life. Several persons are associated to create something, without which such type of efforts would not be possible. I would like to thanks my parents who have brought me to this world & continuously blessed me to make me an able person in the society. The cover page, the fascination of a book is designed by my eldest daughter Samanwita. My youngest daughter Samapika, also inspired me otherwise, which cannot be denied. Many others who have helped me, both professionally & personally in writing this book also need acknowledgement. I am thankful to google for providing treasure of information to write this book. Last but not the least, I thank God for his enormous blessings.

SUDHIR

CONTENTS

PREFACE

Investment in blue chips companies yielded superior returns in long term as compared to other investment options. The longer time, the money is invested in stock market or equity, it gives a better potential to generate higher income. Investing is all about managing risk & reward. No one can ascertain, where the market moves at any particular time. The tradeoff between risk and reward provides profit & loss to the investor. The profit from the stock market very often endowed with inflation adjusted returns.

Bulls & bears are two market participants; fought between each other and consequently imbalance the demand & supply. The demand & supply are the two driving forces in stock market and responsible for the stock price movement in different directions. Due to some positive or negative news flow, there could be high demand & supply for a particular stock. Sentiment drives demand & supply, consequently stock price.

Thus, timing the market is a difficult task for the investors & traders and very often the market participants fail to predict the right directions. Instead of timing the market, one alternative strategy has been formulated, i.e., Dollar Cost Averaging, which can be conducive for the investors at all levels. This book is written for educational purposes only. The profit & loss is trader's responsibility.

INTRODUCTION

In stock market, investors keep accumulating quality stocks in phased manner and reap the benefits of compounding in long term. In short term, the stock market and stock prices are affected by news, rumour & human emotions. Stock prices rise & fall by emotions of market participants. Every adverse news across the globe affects the rest of the world in one or other way. Thus, slightest of the people's sentiment adversely affects the stock market as a whole. The global news spread like wild fire and people start panic selling or buying depending upon the sentiments. Thus, Indian markets take cues from foreign markets; specifically Asian markets, European markets & American markets.

As told by Benjamin Graham, the father of value investing, the market behaves like a voting machine in short term and a weighing machine in long term. Votes are based on sentiments of common people during election period and the market simulates like an election contest in short term. Sentiments of fickle minded people can change instantly and it is difficult to measure accurately. A voting machine counts votes. Thus, in short term, Market has been described as voting machine. But in long term, the market behaves rationally being more precise and accurate like a weighing machine, measuring the weight accurately.

Hence, it is desirable that investors should invest for the long term. In long term, the stock price usually appreciate in value and bring forth profits to the investors. To avoid untoward situations and misfiring during one time entry, it is advisable to accumulate the stocks gradually. The gradual accumulation of stocks, preferably of fixed amount call forth the concept of Dollar Cost Averaging.

THE POWER OF COMPOUNDING

Albert Einstein told, Compounding Interest as world's eighth wonder. When people start investing, it is imperative to understand how compounding works and affects the investments. People start thinking about financial matter quite late in life. The finest way to exploit the effects of compounding is to start investing early. An early start of investing something would bring forth the investor a high up compounding effect. Over time, the small but regular investment snowballs in to a substantial amount; building a great corpus. The magic of compounding works only with long term investment. The power of compounding is responsible for generating enormous wealth, if right asset is choosen. When someone regularly accumulate something, over time it is manifested in multiple folds, at a much faster pace.

Compounding requires careful planning & patience so as to grow wealth exponentially. The power of compounding is homologous to rapid multiplication and increasing population. With passage of time, the investors could gain returns and regenerate returns over the yields, thus guiding to increase the investment quickly.

Equity investments have greater potential to make over better returns over long term, besides other investment options including inflation adjustment. Young chaps often ignore to save for retirement. Considering the future horizon to be far reaching, people stressed upon other expenses more urgent and mistreated investment exposure. Small & continuous savings in long run, pay off enormously someday; much greater than accumulating bigger amounts in later stages. As soon as the first salary is received, it is imperative to make investing before other expenditure. Compounding is a strategy, that makes money work for the investors. By investing regularly, the investors can keep the portfolio healthy.

However, the power of compounding is not limited to just the compound interest, but it is a skillful handling of assets to create wealth. Creating wealth is an art in which time value is harnessed to proliferate the pin money to make big bucks.

FUNDAMENTALS OF CALL & PUT

Call & Put are two essential elements of future & option contract. A call option gives the buyer the right but not the obligation to buy the underlying stock at a specific price called the strike price and within a set period of time called Expiration Period. To buy a call, the buyer has to pay premium. Call option buyers pay premium and Call option sellers collects premium. For Call option buyers, if the market goes up; there will be profit. Conversely, for Call option sellers if the market goes down; there will be profit. Thus, if the underlying is anticipated to rise, buy a call option and if the underlying is anticipated to fall, sell a call option.

A put gives the buyer the right but not the obligation to sell the underlying stock at a specific price called the strike price and within a set period of time called Expiration Period. To buy a put, the buyer has to pay premium. Put option buyers pay premium and Put option sellers collects premium. For Put option buyers, if the market goes down; there will be profit. Conversely, for Put option sellers if the market goes up; there will be profit. Thus, if the underlying is anticipated to fall, buy a put option and if the underlying is anticipated to rise, sell a put option.

Option sellers have obligations while options buyers have rights. Option buyers are provided with freedom to trade the contracts without being imposed by anyone. Conversely, Option sellers are imposed with obligation to trade the contracts if the buyers decide to exercise the options. The option buyers have to pay the premium to the option sellers for carrying all the risks that is with the obligations. Thus option buyers have to pay the premium and option sellers keep the premium with them. Premium is basically a fee which is paid for buying an option. Option premium depends upon Strike Price, Time to Expiration & Underlying Volatility. The price at which the security must be traded between the buyer & seller when the option is exercised, is called

Strike Price. Whenever an investor chooses to sell or purchase the underlying shares, it is known as "Exercising the Option". The stock price must cross above the strike price for calls and below the strike price for puts before expiry so that an option will be exercised and profitable. If the option is never exercised, the seller pockets the premium. Options derive their value from the underlying asset or stocks. Hence it is called as derivative.

The premium of a call or put option is the price of that option, which the traders or investors pay if they are a buyer or the price which they receive if they are the sellers in executing an options contract. It is just like a booking amount to buy an asset at a future date.

Every Stock & Index included in F & O groups are traded in derivative market with specific lot sizes. Different stocks have different lot sizes. There are selected blue chips stocks in Future & Option list of different Stock exchanges.

It is evident that, due to call & put transactions, the stock prices move up or down. If the underlying stock price moves up, it implies that traders tend to buy more calls or sell more puts. If the underlying stock price moves down, it implies that traders tend to buy more puts or sell more calls.

BROAD OUTLINES OF DOLLAR COST AVERAGING

The traders & investors selected stocks considering the fundamental & technical analysis having Price Earnings Ratio (P/E ratio) less than 15, Earnings Per Share (EPS) & Return on Equity (ROE) greater than 20 etc. and so on. The blue chips companies are stable and most companies provide dividends consistently for 10-20 yrs. with consistently increasing earnings for 5 consecutive years, increasing trend of sales per shares having limited debt are considered for investing. However, sometimes the selected stocks may not satisfy all the criteria during screening. One cannot predict the right direction of the market and thus, cannot choose the right stocks always.

Thus, the retail investors should always select few stocks preferably from the Nifty 50 or BSE 30 list. The selection of stocks may be from the F & O list; in case of non-success to make strategy for stock repair.

Select one or two stocks from each sector and accumulate them gradually. The stock should be of market leader.

The retail investors are small & medium sized, having small capital to invest. From the monthly pay-cheque or business income, investors invest some amount as monthly savings for future requirements. The amount may be lump sum or fixed amount in regular interval. Gradually, the savings accumulated in to a large amount and fulfills the need of the investor. It is a disciplined way of investing for the future need.

With greater number of investments in shape of quantity or amount accumulated over long period, the investors benefit from the incremental stock price movements and accumulated dividends. Having accumulated stocks equivalent to its lot size in derivative segment, suitable options strategy can be established to make regular income.

Dollar Cost Averaging is a way for investors of putting fixed amount of money in to an investment on regular basis, despite market conditions. Ignoring predictions on stock price movements, this strategy indulge in making investment consistently. Stock prices are subject to wide fluctuation in a trending market. Dollar Cost Averaging is the best way to tackle such situation.

Dollar Cost Averaging helps investors to begin investing with small amount of capital. Some investor may not have large sum of capital to invest all at once, thus miss out potential gains. But, dollar cost averaging smoothes out ups & downs of the market. Passive investors, who are unable to track the market regularly may find dollar cost averaging as panacea. They can stay committed to the investment discipline and do away with emotion.

CONCEPT OF DOLLAR COST AVERAGING

Dollar Cost Averaging is the investing practice of fixed amount in shape of Dollar or Rupee or any other currency on a regular basis, irrespective of stock price. The stock price moves up & down in the face of people's sentiment. Instead of buying at one go with lump sum amount, the investors usually prefer to enable the dollar cost averaging and take advantage, most likely of price decline. The dollar cost averaging thus reduces the average cost price per share. Frequent & regular investment over a long period of time make investors less likely to miss out several buying opportunities.

The novice investors don't have larger amount of money to invest in stock market. Dollar Cost Averaging pass on smaller amounts of investment in to the market at regular interval. In such fashion, the investors don't have to wait to accumulate larger amount of fund to invest in the market. Even if they have some money, they lack of knowledge, where to invest, when to invest and how to invest. Dollar Cost Averaging is thus a lay man concept for the novice investors to start the journey of stock market.

In stock market it cannot be exactly predicted and caught the top & bottom of a stock. It is also unpredictable, how far a stock price may plunged or surged. The low price of today could be a relatively high price of tomorrow and the high price of today could be a relatively low price in tomorrow. The stock prices tend to rise over the long run, but do not rise consistently over the near term. Thus, Dollar Cost Averaging works over the long term. There are other benefits to consider for dollar cost averaging besides reducing the cost per share. It instills a good investing habbits to accumulate huge quantity of stocks. The market opportunities can be opened for a prolonged periods depending upon the capital available with the investor. The investors are endowed with the opportunities to enter in to the stock market, when they knock.

Stocks offer superior growth potential and outperformed other forms of investment in the long term; if purchased the right stocks at the right time. When the investor has invested a large sum of money in a single trade and the stock price go south, the investor may feel regret. Gradual accumulation may not harm more to a investor due to the effects of dollar cost averaging.

The investors & traders inclined to be affected more strongly to losses than to profits. When smaller amount is invested over a period of time, the pitfalls of unsuccessful investing is scared off. The Dollar Cost Averaging makes it conducive to ward off the market uncertainty by systematic and automated investment.

Dollar Cost Averaging strategy helps investors to keep off from the wrath of sudden fluctuation of stock prices. Buying all the stocks at one go using the available resources is quite risky. Such incremental accumulation set forth the investors likelihood of dividing the risk. Consequent upon, even if the market put up with disruption; eventually the investment be impacted in that particular period. That means, only a small part be affected and saved the investors from losses.

Giving way to regular investments with a fixed value each time, it will be accumulated more of the shares when stock prices are falling and less of the shares when stock prices are increasing. As such the investors buy more shares when the cost is low, thus reducing the average cost per share over time. Over the long term, dollar cost averaging can help lower the investment cost and boost the returns.

The most significant dollar cost averaging example in India is GPF/PPF contribution, Mutual Fund SIP and Bank or Post Office Recurring Deposits etc. The salary holders employees invest on monthly basis, a compulsory deduction from salary as a contribution towards GPF/PPF. Individual investors invest in different mutual funds, irrespective of present market scenario with a fixed amount as SIP. Most of the general investors, who are unaware about the mutual fund or stock market; invest in bank or post office as recurring deposits.

Dollar Cost Averaging is the practice of investing the same amount at regular intervals. Investors who are consistently putting money in to the market as dollar cost average may seen their portfolio dropping initially. But, with the passage of time, when market started to recover, the stock price would have steadily increased higher.

Example:

The investment of Rs. 3,00,000/- in stock market using dollar cost averaging can be accomplished in 12 months by investing @ Rs. 25000/- per month in gradual manners. The table shown below depicts the trades for lump sum investment as well as dollar cost averaging strategy.

Sl. No.	Month	Lump Sum purchase of Rs. 3 Lakh		Dollar Cost Averaging of Rs. 25000/ monthly	
		Stock Price	No. of shares purchased	Stock Price	No. of shares purchased
1	January	100	3000	100	250.00
2	February			99	252.50
3	March			98	255.10
4	April			97	257.70
5	May			96	260.40
6	June			92	271.75
7	July			89	280.90
8	August			96	260.40
9	September			100	250.00
10	October			102	245.10
11	November			104	240.40
12	December			106	235.85
Total Share purchased			3000		3060
Average share price		100		98.25	

With a lump sum investment of Rs. 3 lakh, the investor can purchase 3000 stocks @ of Rs. 100 per stock. However, under dollar cost averaging, the investors can purchase 3060 stocks @ Rs. 98.25 each. Therefore, dollar cost averaging can provide increased number of shares when the market is declining and provide less number of shares if the market is rising.

Dollar Cost Averaging is one of the good way to flourish a disciplined investing habbit. Dollar Cost Averaging in shape of fixed amount may provide fractional shares, but now various brokers have come about to allow customers to purchase fractional shares of stock, making dollar cost averaging much easier and comfortable.

Dollar Cost Averaging in the process reduces investment risk and thereby preserved the capital. The emotional roller coaster in accumulating the shares is minimized over a long period of time. The investor may use this strategy for any investment, whether it is stock (must be blue chips companies), mutual funds (Top rated MF) or exchange traded funds like nifty bee, bank bee, gold bee or silver bee etc.

Before adopting dollar cost averaging, it is to be ascertained, how much money the investor want to invest and how often he want to invest. Weekly, Monthly or Quarterly interval may be selected to adopt this strategy as per the fund & conducive market conditions. Bear market is more conducive than bull market, but the investment must be in a blue chips company. Those investors, who remain invested during market declines might have seen better returns as compared to those who have withdrawn capital and try to time a market return. Historically, it has been seen.

The stock market tends to move in cycles of up & down. But, the stocks have inherent upward bias in long run. When stock price goes down, investor very often gets fearful and sell. When stock price goes up, investor might be tempted to buy more in euphoria. Dollar Cost

Averaging is most effective in down trending market, due to buying more shares at lower prices.

Dollar Cost Averaging is more suitable for investors being concerned with minimization of risk than earning huge profits. However, the investment performance depends more on the stocks selected for investment.

When the investor invest at frequent intervals, the risk is being distributed over a period of time keeping at bay with the bad market timing. This significant strategy of Dollar Cost Averaging was first enunciated by Benjamin Graham, the father of value investing in his book "The Intelligent Investor" in 1949. The excerpt well written as follows:

"The practitioner invests in common stocks the same number of dollars each month or each quarter. In this way he buys more shares when the market is low than when it is high, and he is likely to end up with a satisfactory overall price for all his holdings".

DOLLAR COST AVERAGING STRATEGY
DISCUSSION

Investing in stock is one of the greatest methods of appreciating the investment to a multi-bagger status. Multi bagger is a concept of appreciating an investment in to a many fold growth. The stock investors endowed with lifetime opportunity to earn without hard working. Stocks work for the investors, when they are sleeping. In India, very few percentage of people are involved in stock market. It is due to the fact that, most of the traders or investors are facing irreparable loss during their first entry in to the stock market. People don't go through the pros & cons of the stock market and dive in to the oblivion with other people's tips. Thus, blame the stock market and disregard.

Dollar Cost Averaging is usually made in stock market with blue chips stocks. If the investors are making dollar cost averaging using bad off stocks, the performance will be gloomy. The future prediction of a specific stock might be wrong and investing lump sum amount in stock at the wrong time may incur huge losses. Keeping in view, dollar cost averaging manage to minimize risk in long run.

Market declines may panic investors, but dollar cost averaging can help investors to keep in track of investment and potentially lowering the investment cost. It helps gradually to build up the holdings of a particular stock over a period of time. Dollar Cost Averaging is an ideal strategy for novice investors, who is in dream of building a long term portfolio.

Dollar Cost Averaging takes over emotions out of investing and prevents from potentially damaging the portfolio and consequent stock return. The automated investment of fixed amount over regular intervals of time make methods favourable to purchase stocks under pressure in volatile market. This system is specifically useful for novice investors, who don't have any experience or expertise in judging the most opportune time to buy.

Most people are saving & investing as they earn money. The salaried individuals who have regular income every month may opt for dollar cost averaging with stocks or systematic investment plan with ETFs or Mutual Funds. Buying low and selling high in stock market may not be always possible and the investors wait for long time to recoup the losses. The stocks moving lower tend to move further low and the stocks moving higher tend to move further high. Investing one time in to the market may be detrimental if the stock price moves unidirectional, contrarily.

Very often, when market declines, investors become afraid and panic sell. Dollar Cost Averaging of superior company may give profit in long term. Blue Chips companies bounce back early and recover the losses.

The investor might consider dollar cost averaging if he is beginning to invest and having smaller amounts to buy shares. Sometimes, the investors buy at high prices and sometimes at low prices. But, the process helps investing in a disciplined way. This process rarely produces better results than lump sum investing, but conducive for investors with lower risk tolerance.

Dollar Cost Averaging may not be fruitful in assuring profit or protecting loss in the face of a declining market, where the stock price drops dramatically. The limitation in investing a lump sum amount in purchasing a stock or mutual fund or ETF lies when the price of the asset drops continuously; consequently reducing the entire lump sum value. In such case, dollar cost averaging comes to the rescue.

Lump sum investing is a risky plan of action due to highly unknown time ahead. Conversely, investors break down the available capital in to smaller parts and buy fixed amount at regular intervals. Irrespective of stock price movement, investors keep going investing. Thus, they avoid predicting future price movements.

Though dollar cost averaging is less risky, it gives moderate return to the investors. The main loopholes in dollar cost averaging is that, the investors used to buy shares even when it is not favourable to accumulate.

MUTUAL FUND & SYSTEMATIC INVESTMENT PLAN

A mutual fund is a company that pools together money from different investors and invest such large pool of money in a selected portfolio of stocks. Every Mutual Fund is managed by professional fund manager who look after the money of small investors and invests in appropriate sectors for steady growth. Mutual funds usually invest in a wide variety of companies & industries which simulate diversification of portfolio and synonymous with the age old wall street adage " Don't put all your eggs in one basket".

The Indian Mutual Fund offers various schemes to cater all types of investor needs. Mutual Fund is one of the safest ways for novice investors to invest money in Stock Market. Mutual Funds are not traded in any stock exchange like stocks or ETFs. Very small amount of money as low as Rs. 500/- is required to start an investment in Mutual Fund. At the beginning stage when the investor has not enough idea about stock market and the investor has not enough time to make research on stocks, investing through Mutual Fund is a great idea which can be purchased through SIP (Systematic Investment Plan) on monthly basis or purchasing one time investment of some units of Mutual Fund for a fixed amount; say Rs. 5000/- or more.

SIP is mostly suitable for regular (low & middle) income group. The required Nos. unit of Mutual Fund can be calculated by dividing the amount by its NAV (Net Asset Value). SIP is the systematic deposit of fixed amount of money per month in Mutual Funds. SIP investment is better than a one-time Lump Sum investment as percentage of loss is minimized and averaged during the down trend. Generally, Mutual Fund charges some fees while making transactions during buying & selling. Fees charged during purchasing of MF are called Entry Load and fees charged during selling of MF is called Exit load.

Systematic Investment Plan helps mutual fund investors in investing systematic way aside from taking in to account the market volatility & timing. It uses capital to accumulate assets in a disciplined way over time. The compounding effects of SIP & benefits can be visualized through regular investing for long term. SIP is synonymous with the dollar cost averaging.

COVERED CALL STRATEGY

Covered Call strategy involves selling of an higher strike price call option with respect to a long position in the same stock or asset at lower level. During the life time of the sold call option, the investors or traders anticipates a minor change in the underlying stock price.

It is usually said covered when the investors or traders are selling call options against the existing underlying stock position. The word 'covered' signifies that the position is protected from unlimited risk. Covered Call strategy is established with up trending stocks having mild to moderately bullish outlook. In this strategy, traders simultaneously buy 1 lot stock & sell 1 OTM call. This is one limited profit and limited risk strategy, in which upside is fully protected and down side is partly protected; limited to the level equivalent to the premium received by selling of the call option. When the investors or traders are selling options, they generally want to have as little time as possible to be wrong. The rate of time decay increases as the expiration time approaches. Hence, this strategy is suitable for short term expiration to take advantages of accelerating time decay.

Example - 1

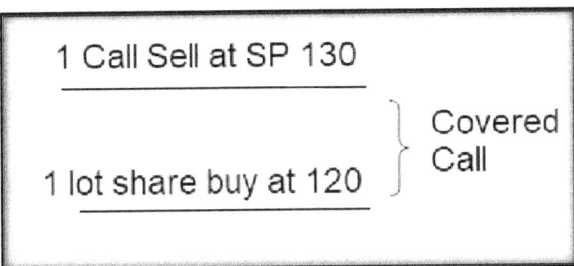

Suppose the stock is trading at Rs. 120/- and sentiment of market is mild to moderately bullish and the investors want to initiate a Covered Call strategy with some F & O stock, say Tata Steel. To establish a covered call strategy, the investors have to buy 1 lot share of stock at current market price, say at Rs. 120/- and simultaneously selling 1 Call option at strike price of 130 @ Rs. 6.00. By selling the call option at Strike

Price of 130, the investor will receive a premium of Rs. 6.00.

<u>Analysis of profit & loss at various levels:-</u>

For buying stock at spot price 120, you have to pay Rs. 120 per share.

For 130 Call option 1 lot sell, premium received = Rs. 6/-

Net debit = 6 − 120 = (-) Rs. 114/- (Debit)

The overall cash flow of the strategy at different expiry level:

Case 1 – Market expires at 100 (below the buy price of stock)

   i. The long stock position will be in loss of Rs. = 20/-.

   ii. Strike Price 130 sold call will expire worthless & we keep the entire premium of Rs. 6/-.

   iii. Total Loss = - 20 + 6 = (-) Rs. 14/- multiplied by Lot Size = -14 x 5500 = (-) Rs. 77000/-

Case 2 - Market expires at 110 (below the buy price of stock)

    i. The long stock position will be in loss of Rs. = 10/-.

    ii. Strike Price 130 sold call will expire worthless & we keep the entire premium of Rs. 6/-.

    iii. Total Loss = - 10 + 6 = (-) Rs. 4/- multiplied by Lot Size = - 4 x 5500 = (-) Rs. 22000/-

Case 3 - Market expires at 114 (Break Even Point = Stock buy price - Net Credit)

    i. The long stock position will be in loss of Rs. = 6/-

    ii. Strike Price 130 sold call will expire worthless & we keep the entire premium of Rs. 6/-.

    iii. Total Loss = - 6 + 6 = 0; multiplied by Lot Size = 0 x 5500 = Zero.

Case 4 - Market expires at 120 (at the buy price of stock)

    i. The long stock position will be in no loss no profit.

ii. Strike Price 130 sold call will expire worthless & we keep the entire premium of Rs. 6/-.

iii. Total Profit = Rs. 6/- multiplied by Lot Size = 6 x 5500 = Rs. 33000/-

Case 5 - Market expires at 130 (at the sold price of option)

i. The long stock position will be in profit of Rs. = 10/-.

ii. Strike Price 130 sold call will expire worthless & we keep the entire premium of Rs. 6/-.

iii. Total Profit = 10 + 6 = Rs. 16/- multiplied by Lot Size = 16 x 5500 = Rs. 88000/-

Case 6 - Market expires at 140 (above the sold price of option)

i. The long stock position will be in profit of Rs. = 20/-.

ii. Strike Price 130 sold call will be assigned & in loss of Rs. 10/-; The net payoff will be − 10 + 6 = (-) Rs. 4/-.

iii. Total Profit = 20 - 4 = Rs. 16/- multiplied by Lot

Size = 16 x 5500 = Rs. 88000/-

Summary in Tabular Form:

Sl. No.	Items	Stock Closing Price at Expiry						Remarks
		100	110	114	120	130	140	
1	Credit/ Debit received	(- 120 + 6) = (–) Rs. 114						Debit
2	Payout from Long Stock at 120	100	110	114	120	130	140	
3	Payout from Short Call SP 130	0	0	0	0	0	- 10	
4	Net Payoff	- 14	-4	0	6	16	16	
5	Profit/ Loss	- 77000	- 22000	0	33000	88000	88000	Lot Size = 5500

In making this strategy of Covered Call,

Max Profit = Premium Received + (Strike Price of Short

Call - Purchase Price of Underlying) - Commissions

= 6.00 + (130-120) = 16.00 x (Lot size of stock i.e., 5500) - Commissions

Max Profit Achieved When Price of Underlying >= Strike Price of Short Call,

i.e., when the stock price is greater than equal to 130.

Maximum Profit = 88,000/-

Down side is partly protected; limited to the level equivalent to the premium received by selling the call option. Hence up to (Purchase price of stock – premium received) level, the strategy is protected. i.e., 120 – 6.00 = 114.00 level.

Loss Occurs When Price of Underlying < Purchase Price of Underlying - Premium Received,

i.e., losses starts increasing and are unlimited when the stock price falls below (120 – 6.00 = 114.00) level.

Maximum Loss = Unlimited

Breakeven Point = Purchase Price of Underlying - Premium Received i.e., 120 – 6.00 = 114.00, the level at which no profit, no loss.

i.e. When the stock price increases above purchase price, i.e. 120 level, Profit begins and start increasing. Maximum profit will be achieved at 130 levels. After crossing 130 levels, no further profit will be gained. Above 130 levels, the losses from short call will be offset by the gain from stock appreciation. Whatever may be the expiry level above 130, maximum profit will be Rs. 16.00 x 5500 = 88,000/-

When the stock price falls below 114.00 level, Loss will be occurred and start increasing. Maximum Loss will be unlimited below 114.00 levels.

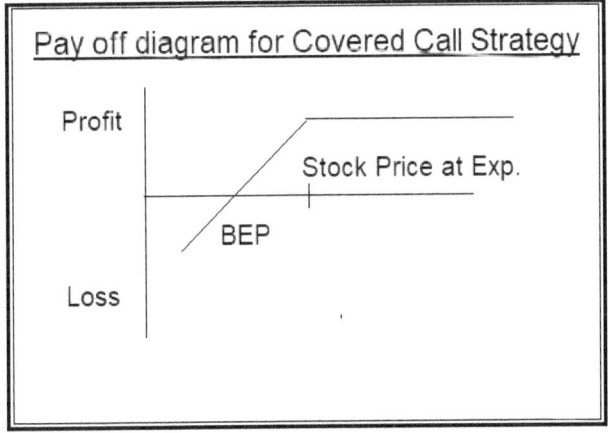

Pay off diagram for Covered Call Strategy

Example – 2

```
┌─────────────────────────────────────┐
│  ┌────────────────────────────┐     │
│   1 Call Sell at SP 130             │
│  ────────────────────────           │
│                           ⎫ Covered │
│   1 lot share buy at 110  ⎬ Call    │
│  ────────────────────────  ⎭        │
│                                     │
└─────────────────────────────────────┘
```

Suppose someone has bought 1 lot share of some F & O stock at Rs. 110/- and now the stock is trading at Rs. 120/-. The investor or trader is in profit of Rs. 10/-. If it is felt that, the sentiment of market is mild to moderately bullish and the investors want to initiate a Covered Call strategy against the existing stock. To establish a covered call, the investors have to sold 1 Call option at higher strike price (suppose at 130). By selling the call option at Strike Price of 130, the investor will receive a premium of Rs. 6.00.

Analysis of profit & loss at various levels:-

For buying stock at spot price 110, you have to pay Rs. 110 per share.

For 130 Call option 1 lot sell, premium received = Rs. 6/-

Net debit = 6 – 110 = (-) Rs. 104/- (Debit)

The overall cash flow of the strategy at different expiry level:

Case 1 – Market expires at 100 (below the buy price of stock)

    i. The long stock position will be in loss of Rs. = 10/-.

    ii. Strike Price 130 sold call will expire worthless & we keep the entire premium of Rs. 6/-.

    iii. Total Loss = - 10 + 6 = (-) Rs. 4/- multiplied by Lot Size = - 4 x 5500 = (-) Rs. 22000/-

Case 2 - Market expires at 104 (Break Even Point = Stock bought price - Net Credit)

    i. The long stock position will be in loss of Rs. = 6/-

    ii. Strike Price 130 sold call will expire worthless & we keep the entire premium of Rs. 6/-.

iii. Total Loss = - 6 + 6 = 0; multiplied by Lot Size = 0 x 5500 = Zero.

Case 3 - Market expires at 110 (at the buy price of stock)

    i.   The long stock position will be in no loss no profit = Zero

    ii. Strike Price 130 sold call will expire worthless & we keep the entire premium of Rs. 6/-.

    iii. Total Profit = + 6 = Rs. 6/- multiplied by Lot Size = 6 x 5500 = Rs. 33000/-

Case 4 - Market expires at 120 (above the buy price of stock)

    i.   The long stock position will be in profit of Rs. 10/-

    ii. Strike Price 130 sold call will expire worthless & we keep the entire premium of Rs. 6/-.

    iii. Total Profit = Rs. (10 + 6) multiplied by Lot Size = 16 x 5500 = Rs. 88,000/-

Case 5 - Market expires at 130 (at the sold price of option)

   i. The long stock position will be in profit of Rs. = 20/-.

   ii. Strike Price 130 sold call will expire worthless & we keep the entire premium of Rs. 6/-.

   iii. Total Profit = 20 + 6 = Rs. 26/- multiplied by Lot Size = 26 x 5500 = Rs. 1,43,000/-

Case 6 - Market expires at 140 (above the sold price of option)

   i. The long stock position will be in profit of Rs. = 30/-.

   ii. Strike Price 130 sold call will be assigned & in loss of Rs. 10/-; The net payoff will be – 10 + 6 = (-) Rs. 4/-.

   iii. Total Profit = 30 - 4 = Rs. 26/- multiplied by Lot Size = 26 x 5500 = Rs. 1,43,000/-

Summary in Tabular Form:

Sl. No.	Items	Stock Closing Price at Expiry						Remarks
		100	104	110	120	130	140	

1	Credit/ Debit received	(- 110 + 6) = (–) Rs. 104						Debit
2	Payout from Long Stock at 110	100	104	110	120	130	140	
3	Payout from Short Call SP 130	0	0	0	0	0	- 10	
4	Net Payoff	- 4	0	6	16	26	26	
5	Profit/ Loss	- 77000	0	33000	88000	143000	143000	Lot Size = 5500

In making this strategy of Covered Call,

Max Profit = Premium Received + (Strike Price of Short

Call - Purchase Price of Underlying) - Commissions

= 6.00 + (130-110) = 26.00 x (Lot size of stock i.e.,

5500) - Commissions

Max Profit Achieved When Price of Underlying >= Strike

Price of Short Call,

i.e., when the stock price is greater than equal to 130.

Maximum Profit = 1,43,000/-

Down side is partly protected; limited to the level equivalent to the premium received by selling the call option. Hence up to (Purchase price of stock – premium received) level, the strategy is protected. i.e., 110 – 6.00 = 104.00 level.

Loss Occurs When Price of Underlying < Purchase Price of Underlying - Premium Received,

i.e., losses are unlimited when the stock price falls below (110 – 6.00 = 104.00) level.

Maximum Loss = Unlimited

Breakeven Point = Purchase Price of Underlying - Premium Received

i.e., 110 – 6.00 = 104.00, the level at which no profit, no loss.

During establishment of Covered Call strategy, there was initial profit of Rs. 10 x 5500 = Rs. 55,000/-. If the stock price start increasing. Maximum profit will be achieved at 130 levels. After crossing 130 levels, no further profit will be gained. Above 130 levels, the losses from short call will offset by the gain from stock appreciation. Whatever may be the expiry level above 130, maximum profit will be Rs. 26.00 x 5500 = 1,43,000/-

When the stock price falls below 104.00 level, Loss will be occurred and start increasing. Maximum Loss will be unlimited below 104.00 levels.

Example - 3

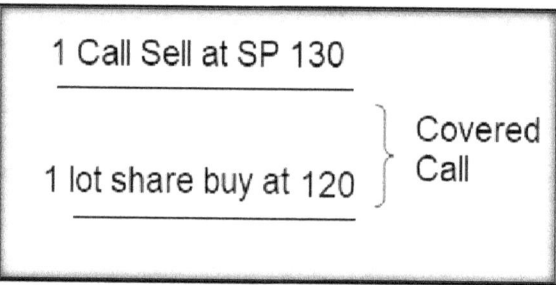

Suppose someone has bought 1 lot share of some F & O stock, say Tata Steel at Rs. 120/- and now the stock is trading at Rs. 110/-. The investor or trader is in loss of Rs. 10/-. If it is felt that, the sentiment of market is mild to moderately bullish and the investors want to initiate a Covered Call strategy against the existing stock. To establish a covered call, the investors have to sold 1 Call option at higher strike price (suppose at 130). By selling the call option at Strike Price of 130, the investor will receive a premium of Rs. 4.00.

<u>Analysis of profit & loss at various levels:-</u>

For buying stock at spot price 120, you have to pay Rs. 120 per share.

For 130 Call option 1 lot sell, premium received = Rs. 4/-

Net debit = 4 – 120 = (-) Rs. 116/- (Debit)

The overall cash flow of the strategy at different expiry level:

Case 1 – Market expires at 100 (below the buy price of stock)

i. The long stock position will be in loss of Rs. = 20/-.

ii. Strike Price 130 sold call will expire worthless & we keep the entire premium of Rs. 4/-.

iii. Total Loss = - 20 + 4 = (-) Rs. 16/- multiplied by Lot Size = -16 x 5500 = (-) Rs. 88000/-

Case 2 - Market expires at 110 (below the buy price of stock)

    i. The long stock position will be in loss of Rs. = 10/-.

    ii. Strike Price 130 sold call will expire worthless & we keep the entire premium of Rs. 4/-.

    iii. Total Loss = - 10 + 4 = (-) Rs. 6/- multiplied by Lot Size = - 6 x 5500 = (-) Rs. 33000/-

Case 3 - Market expires at 116 (Break Even Point = Stock bought price - Net Credit)

    i. The long stock position will be in loss of Rs. = 4/-

    ii. Strike Price 120 sold call will expire worthless & we keep the entire premium of Rs. 4/-.

    iii. Total Loss = - 4 + 4 = 0; multiplied by Lot Size = 0 x 5500 = Zero.

Case 4 - Market expires at 120 (at the buy price of stock)

   i. The long stock position will be in no loss no profit.

   ii. Strike Price 130 sold call will expire worthless & we keep the entire premium of Rs. 4/-.

   iii. Total Profit = Rs. 4/- multiplied by Lot Size = 4 x 5500 = Rs. 22000/-

Case 5 - Market expires at 130 (at the sold price of option)

   i. The long stock position will be in profit of Rs. = 10/-.

   ii. Strike Price 130 sold call will expire worthless & we keep the entire premium of Rs. 4/-.

   iii. Total Profit = 10 + 4 = Rs. 14/- multiplied by Lot Size = 14 x 5500 = Rs. 77,000/-

Case 6 - Market expires at 140 (above the sold price of option)

i. The long stock position will be in profit of Rs. = 20/-.

ii. Strike Price 130 sold call will be in loss of Rs. 10/-; The net payoff will be – 10 + 4 = (-) Rs. 6/-.

iii. Total Profit = 20 - 6 = Rs. 14/- multiplied by Lot Size = 14 x 5500 = Rs. 77,000/-

Summary in Tabular Form:

Sl. No.	Items	Stock Closing Price at Expiry						Remarks
		100	110	116	120	130	140	
1	Credit/ Debit received	(- 120 + 4) = (–) Rs. 116						Debit
2	Payout from Long Stock at 120	100	110	116	120	130	140	
3	Payout from Short Call SP 130	0	0	0	0	0	- 10	
4	Net Payoff	- 16	- 6	0	4	14	14	
5	Profit/ Loss	-88000	-33000	0	22000	77000	77000	Lot Size = 5500

In making this strategy of Covered Call,

Max Profit = Premium Received + (Strike Price of Short Call - Purchase Price of Underlying) - Commissions

= 4.00 + (130-120) = 14.00 x (Lot size of stock i.e., 5500) – Commissions.

Max Profit Achieved When Price of Underlying >= Strike Price of Short Call,

i.e., when the stock price is greater than equal to 130.

Maximum Profit = 77,000/-

Down side is partly protected; limited to the level equivalent to the premium received by selling the call option. Hence up to (Purchase price of stock – premium received) level, the strategy is protected. i.e., 120 – 4.00 = 116.00 level.

Loss Occurs When Price of Underlying < Purchase Price of Underlying - Premium Received,

i.e., losses are unlimited when the stock price falls below (120 – 4.00 = 116.00) level.

Maximum Loss = Unlimited

Breakeven Point = Purchase Price of Underlying - Premium Received

i.e., 120 – 4.00 = 116.00, the level at which no profit, no loss.

i.e. When the stock price increases above purchase price, i.e. 120 level, Profit begins and start increasing. Maximum profit will be achieved at 130 levels. After crossing 130 levels, no further profit will be gained. Above 130 levels, the losses from short call will offset by the gain from stock appreciation. Whatever may be the expiry level above 130, maximum profit will be Rs. 14.00 x 5500 = 77,000/-

When the stock price falls below 116.00 level, Loss will be occurred and start increasing. Maximum Loss will be unlimited below 116.00 levels.

From the above three examples, it is construed that, covered call will be profitable, if the stock price is mild to moderately bullish.

Covered call may be established with OTM, ATM or ITM call options, depending upon the risk appetite and market sentiments. In covered call strategy, there is a tradeoff between higher profit & higher level of protection. There is a higher level of protection in ITM covered call, thus lower profitability. In case of OTM covered call, there is higher profitability and lower level of protection.

Covered Call with ITM Options:

A Call option is ITM, if the stock price is higher than the option strike price. A Put option is ITM if the stock price is lower than the option strike price. The ITM options have always associated with some intrinsic value & time value. Premium for ITM option is more, thus more lucrative for option selling. Covered call with ITM options provide greater downside protection and larger profit range.

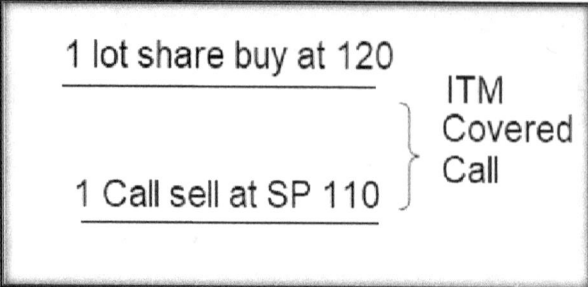

Suppose someone has bought 1 lot share of some F & O stock, say Tata Steel, which is trading at Rs. 120/-. If it is felt that, the sentiment of market is neutral to mildly bullish or bearish and the investors want to initiate a Covered Call strategy. To establish ITM covered call strategy, the investors have to sold 1 Call option at lower strike price (suppose at 110). By selling the ITM call option at Strike Price of 110, the investor will receive a handsome premium of Rs. 11.50.

In this strategy, the investor has to pay Rs. (120 x 5500 = 660000/-) for 1 lot share, say Tata Steel. Simultaneously, he also receives a premium of Rs. (5500 x 11.50 = Rs. 63250/-) due to selling of call option. Thus, the net investment is Rs. (660000 − 63250 = Rs. 596750/-)

Case 1 - If the stock price rises to 130 (above the buying price of stock) at expiration and the call gets assigned:

i. The long stock position will be in profit of Rs. = 10/-.

ii. Strike Price 110 sold call will be assigned & loss will be (-) 20, thus net payoff = (- 20 + 11.50) = (-) Rs. 8.50

iii. Total Profit = 10 – 8.50 = Rs. 1.50 multiplied by Lot Size = 1.50 x 5500 = Rs. 8250/-

Case 2 - If the stock price falls to 110 (at the sold price of option) at expiration:

i. The long stock position will be in loss of Rs. = 10/-.

ii. Strike Price 110 sold call will expire worthless and the trader will keep the entire premium of Rs. 11.50

iii. Total Profit = - 10 + 11.50 = Rs. 1.50 multiplied by Lot Size = 1.50 x 5500 = Rs. 8250/-

Case 3 - If the stock price rises to 140 (much above the buying price of stock) at expiration and the call gets assigned:

i.   The long stock position will be in profit of Rs. = 20/-.

ii. Strike Price 110 sold call will be assigned & loss will be (-) 30, thus net payoff = (- 30 + 11.50) = (-) Rs. 18.50

iii. Total Profit = 20 – 18.50 = Rs. 1.50 multiplied by Lot Size = 1.50 x 5500 = Rs. 8250/-

Case 4 - If the stock price falls to 100 (much below the sold price of option) at expiration:

i.   The long stock position will be in loss of Rs. = 20/-.

ii. Strike Price 110 sold call will expire worthless and the trader will keep the entire premium of Rs. 11.50

iii. Total Loss =   - 20 + 11.50 = (-) Rs. 8.50 multiplied by Lot Size = - 8.50 x 5500 = (-) Rs. 46750/-

It is evident from the above illustrations that, when stock price rises, there is little profit. If stock price falls, the negativity increases.

In ITM covered call strategy, the call writer has agreed to sell the shares to the call buyers at lower strike price than the price paid for buying the stock. Thus, maximum profit is achieved when the stock price is greater than equal to strike price of the short call. Conversely, loss occurs when the stock price is less than the buying price of the stock less premium received; maximum loss being unlimited.

POOR MAN'S COVERED CALL STRATEGY

Covered call strategy be in need of large amount of capital, which the general investors cannot afford. The capital requirement for buying equity in lots is substantially higher than buying a call option. The poor man's covered call strategy also known as synthetic covered call, replicate the structure of a traditional covered call strategy. It uses diagonal spreads of call options and reduces the capital or margin requirement of a traditional covered call by replacing the stock with an ITM call option of long term expiry (far month). The longer dated ITM call option having delta value approaching to 1, analogous to a long stock position at a fraction of the cost. The short call option is OTM and near term expiry. Poor man's covered call strategy is a great way to generate income like traditional covered call with less capital and risk.

The important drawbacks in this strategy is, if the stock price gives wild fluctuation in either direction before expiration. When the stock price moves higher, the long ITM call option increases and short OTM call option limits upside potential. Conversely, if the stock price falls sharply, the short OTM call option decreases and the long ITM call option will also decreases in value. The short option decays more than the long option in short term, which is the essence of the diagonal spread.

Example

Suppose it is felt that, the sentiment of market is mild to moderately bullish and the investors want to initiate a Covered Call strategy. Due to insufficient funds, the traders unable to establish the covered call with long stock & short call. In such situation, the traders opted to establish a poor man's covered call strategy. The investors have to sold 1 Call option (short term) at higher strike price (suppose at 130) and buy 1 Call option (long term) at lower strike price (suppose at 120).

The structure will be as follows:

1 Call sell at SP 130 Feb @ 4

1 Call buy at SP 120 March @ 8

The maximum loss & profit potential and breakeven point cannot be meticulously calculated due to the use of different expiration periods. Inspite of that, the profit, loss & breakeven point can be calculated more or less by using the usual formulas.

Maximum profit is approximately, the difference between the call strike prices less the premium paid to establish the strategy. Maximum loss will be the net premium paid to establish the strategy. The breakeven point is approximately coincides with the level of long call strike price plus net premium paid.

By selling the call option (short term) at Strike Price of 130, the investor will receive a premium of Rs. 4.00. By buying the call option (long term) at lower strike price say 120, , the investor will pay a premium of Rs. 8.00. Thus, the net premium paid is 4 − 8 = (−) Rs. 4/-.

Maximum Profit ≈ Difference between the call strike prices - premium paid,

i.e., (130 − 120) − 4 = Rs. 6 multiplied by lot size = 6 x 5500 = Rs. 33,000/-

Maximum loss = Net premium paid = Rs. 4 multiplied by lot size = 4 x 5500 = (−) Rs. 22,000/-

Breakeven point = long call strike price + net premium paid = 120 + 4 = 124.

Accordingly, the overall cash flow of the strategy at different expiry level is approximately calculated:

Case 1 − Market expires at 100 (below the buy price of call)

i. The Strike Price 120 long call position will reduce in value and may be Rs. 2/- . The net payoff = 2− 8 = (−) 6

ii. Strike Price 130 sold call will expire worthless & the trader will keep the entire premium of Rs. 4/-.

iii. If it is squared off instantly, total Loss may be = - 6 + 4 = - 2 x 5500 = (-) 11000, or else the trader may carry forward to initiate another strategy for next month.

Case 2 - Market expires at 110 (below the buy price of call)

i. The Strike Price 120 long call position will reduce in value and may be Rs. 3/- The net payoff = 3-8 = (-) 5

ii. Strike Price 130 sold call will expire worthless & the trader will keep the entire premium of Rs. 4/-.

iii. If it is square off, total Loss may be = - 5 + 4 = - 1 x 5500 = (-) Rs. 5500/-, or the trader may carry forward to initiate another strategy for next month.

Case 3 - Market expires at 120 (at the buy price of call)

i.   The Strike Price 120 long call position will reduce in value and may be Rs. 4/-. The net payoff = 4-8 = (-) 4

ii. Strike Price 130 sold call will expire worthless & the trader will keep the entire premium of Rs. 4/-.

iii. If it is square off, total Loss may be = - 4 + 4 = 0 x 5500 = zero, or the trader may carry forward to initiate another strategy for next month.

Case 4 - Market expires at 124 (Break Even Point = Lower strike price + Net debit)

i.   The Strike Price 120 long call position will reduce in value and may be of Rs. 4/- . The net payoff = 4-8 = (-) 4

ii. Strike Price 130 sold call will expire worthless & the trader will keep the entire premium of Rs. 4/-.

iii. If it is square off, total Loss may be = - 4 + 4 = 0 x 5500 = zero, or the trader may carry forward to initiate another strategy for next month.

Case 5 - Market expires at 130 (at the sold price of option)

i. The Strike Price 120 long call position will increase in value and may be of Rs. 10/-, The net payoff = 10-8 = 2

ii. Strike Price 130 sold call will expire worthless & the trader will keep the entire premium of Rs. 4/-.

iii. If it is square off, total Profit may be = 2 + 4 = Rs. 6/- multiplied by Lot Size = 6x 5500 = Rs. 33000/-

Case 6 - Market expires at 140 (above the sold price of option)

i. The Strike Price 120 long call position may be in profit of Rs. 10

ii. Strike Price 130 sold call will be assigned will be in loss of Rs. 10/-. The net pay off = Rs. (4 − 10) = (-) Rs. 6/-.

iii. Total Profit = 10 - 6 = Rs. 4/- multiplied by Lot Size = 4 x 5500 = Rs. 22000/-

Down side risk is limited to the level of long call strike price. Further decrease in stock price does not provide further loss. This strategy gives maximum profit at short call strike price (130). Further increase in stock price does not provide further profit. The profits from the long call is offset by the loss from the short call. The advantage of poor man's covered call is to earn similar profits with less capital.

COVERED CALL STRATEGY DISCUSSION

Whether the strategy is in profit or loss at the beginning, it does not matter. But if the stock price moves higher, the strategy will be profitable. However, if the strategy is sitting on profit from the beginning, there is possibility of more profit with increase of stock price. Conversely, if the strategy is sitting on loss at the beginning, there is possibility of less profit with increase in stock price. It is further ascertained that, if the stock price will decrease during the life time of the strategy, there will be loss incurred in this strategy. If the investor is already in profit with the accumulated stock, he may opt to make covered call strategy and keep stop loss at the breakeven point. If the investor has not accumulated any stock, he may make covered call strategy with simultaneous buying of stock and selling of higher strike price call.

Covered Call is the safest option strategy to make considerable profit. It is desirable to buy quality large cap stock (blue chips company) from BSE 30 or Nifty 50 or F & O List. Accumulate 1 lot in demat account. If it is in profit, make covered call strategy to earn money monthly.

Covered call is a risk management strategy to generate monthly income for the investor or trader from their existing portfolio. In this strategy, one call option is sold against the existing long position. The sold call option is usually OTM, but may be ITM or ATM depending upon the existing position. If the options buyers don't exercise the call option and it expires worthless, the traders or investors may continue selling covered calls against the same shares, time & again.

Covered call works better, either in bullish or almost in neutral market condition. Covered call strategy provides limited profits & unlimited loss. The traders and investors may cautiously establish this strategy in the face of low volatility. If the investors predict higher prices, better to hold on to the stocks instead of covered call writing. Conversely, if the investors predict lower prices, it is better to sell the stocks to avoid losses. If stock price increases, profit also increases, but capped as the stock price reaches the strike price of the short call.

This strategy is implemented with first buying the stocks and simultaneously selling the call option. Before expiry of strategy, the underlying stock should not be disposed off to avoid naked call situation. Naked calls are more risky to deal with. Investors generally employed this strategy, who intend to hold the stock for a long period and don't anticipate stock appreciation in near future. The main disadvantage of covered call strategy is the risk of losses in price falling.

During implementation of covered call strategy, it may be ascertained that, the premium collected in selling the call option is lucrative. Farther the option strike price, cheaper is the option premium. The acceptable premium for selling the call option may be 2% of the stock value as per the rule of thumb.

Success in covered call proliferates in selecting the right stocks & suitable strike price. The traders & investors are assuming limited risk in lieu for the premium of sold call option. Losses occur in covered call strategy, when the stock price falls below the breakeven level. The time period around 30-45 days before expiration is selected to establish this strategy so as to reap higher premiums. The strategy may preferably be run till expiration to get the full benefits of time decay. However, may be squared off early to manage risk or free up trading capitals for better opportunities ahead. If favourable, covered call strategy may yield 1% to 2% profits per month.

With dollar cost averaging, the investors accumulated stocks, of his / her choice to the extent of a lot size in F & O segment. It is very often seen that, when some investor or trader established Covered Call strategy with one lot of pre-existing stock or newly acquired stock, stock price declines considerably. The inadequacy of this strategy is that, when stock price falls, this strategy may not be profitable. To overcome this difficulty, the traders may sometimes established covered call strategy (a modified one) with part of the stock. This may not be a fully traditional covered call strategy. But on the way, the traders may accumulate stocks to covered the strategy completely. This may be accomplished in following two ways:

i.   Suppose, some trader have decided to establish a covered call strategy with one F & O stock, say Tata Steel. Now the stock is trading at Rs. 120/-. If it is felt that, the sentiment of market is mild to moderately bullish and the investors want to initiate a Covered Call strategy. To establish covered call strategy, a modified form, the investors have to sold 1 Call option at higher strike price (suppose at 130). By selling the call option at Strike Price of 130, the investor will receive a premium of Rs. 6.00. The Lot size of Tata Steel say 5500. Unlike traditional Covered Call strategy of buying 1 lot stock simultaneously, the traders may make strategy to buy Tata Steel stocks 25% say 1500 Nos. If the stock price decreases, wait & watch. Don't do anything. By and by, if stock price bounce back and surpasses the 1st buying price, be ready to buy 2nd phase and so on. If the stock price consolidates below buy price and does not crosses above during the life time of the option strategy, the trader or investor keeps the premium with him. The details of transactions are as follow.

Sl. No.	Stock Price	No. of Stocks Buy	Cumulative Stock	Weighted Average Price
1	120	1500	1500	120.00
2	116	-		
3	113	-		
4	110	-		
Total		1500		

Analysis of profit & loss at various levels:-

For buying stocks at price of Rs. 120/-, you have to pay Rs. 120/- per share.

For 130 Call option 1 lot sell, premium received = Rs. 6/-

The overall cash flow of the strategy at different expiry level:

Case 1 – Market expires at 98 (below the buy price of stock)

    i. The long stock position will be in loss of Rs. 22/-

    ii. Strike Price 130 sold call will expire worthless & we keep the entire premium of Rs. 6/-.

    iii. Total Loss = - (1500 x 22) + (6 x 5500) = - 33000 + 33000 = Rs. Zero

Case 2 – Market expires at 100 (below the buy price of stock)

    i. The long stock position will be in loss of Rs. 20/-

    ii. Strike Price 130 sold call will expire worthless & the trader will keep the entire premium of Rs. 6/-.

iii. Total Loss = - (1500 x 20) + (6 x 5500) = - 30000 + 33000 = Rs. 3000/-

Case 3 - Market expires at 110 (below the buy price of stock)

i. The long stock position will be in loss of Rs. 10/-

ii. Strike Price 130 sold call will expire worthless & we keep the entire premium of Rs. 6/-.

iii. Total Loss = - (1500 x 10) + (6 x 5500) = - 15000 + 33000 = Rs. 18000/-

Case 4 - Market expires at 120 (at the buy price of stock)

i. The long stock position will be in no loss, no profit.

ii. Strike Price 130 sold call will expire worthless & we keep the entire premium of Rs. 6/-.

iii. Total Profit = - (1500 x 0) + (6 x 5500) = 0 + 33000 = Rs. 33000/-

Case 5 - Market expires at 130 (at the sold price of option)

   i. The long stock position will be in profit of Rs. 10/-

   ii. Strike Price 130 sold call will expire worthless & we keep the entire premium of Rs. 6/-.

   iii. Total Profit = (1500 x 10) + (6 x 5500) = 15000 + 33000 = Rs. 48000/-

Case 6 - Market expires at 140 (above the sold price of option)

   i. The long stock position will be in profit of Rs. = 20/-

   ii. Strike Price 130 sold call will be assigned & in loss of Rs. 10/-; The net payoff will be − 10 + 6 = (-) Rs. 4/-.

   iii. Total Profit = (1500 x 20) - (4 x 5500) = 30000 − 22000 = Rs. 8000/-

Case 7 - Market expires at 142 (above the sold price of option)

i. The long stock position will be in profit of Rs. = 22/-

ii. Strike Price 130 sold call will be assigned & in loss of Rs. 12/-; The net payoff will be – 12 + 6 = (-) Rs. 6/-.

iii. Total Loss / Profit = (1500 x 22) - (6 x 5500)

33000 – 33000 = Rs. Zero

Case 8 - Market expires at 150 (above the sold price of option)

i. The long stock position will be in profit of Rs. = 30/-

ii. Strike Price 130 sold call will be assigned & in loss of Rs. 20/-; The net payoff will be – 20 + 6 = (-) Rs. 14/-.

iii. Total Loss / Profit = (1500 x 30) - (14 x 5500) = 45000 – 77000 = (-) Rs. 32000/-

When the stock price moves explosively away below the buy price or above the call sell price, exit the strategy to avoid loss.

Summary in Tabular Form:

Sl. No.	Items	Stock Closing Price at Expiry								Remarks
		98	100	110	120	130	140	142	150	
1	Profit/ Loss	0	3000	18000	33000	48000	8000	0	-32000	Lot Size = 5500

In making this strategy, Max Profit Achieved When Price of Underlying = Strike Price of Short Call.

Here, both upside & down side is partly protected. When stock price remains away from the short call strike price in either direction, profit decreases. This strategy is more vulnerable in upside than downside, due to less number of shares in buy side. The long stock is inadequate to offset the losses from the short call in case of price rises. There are two breakeven points in this strategy, upper & lower.

ii. Suppose, some trader have decided to establish a covered call strategy with one F & O stock, say Tata

Steel. Now the stock is trading at Rs. 120/-. If it is felt that, the sentiment of market is mild to moderately bullish and the investors want to initiate a Covered Call strategy. To establish covered call strategy, a modified form, the investors have to sold 1 Call option at higher strike price (suppose at 130). By selling the call option at Strike Price of 130, the investor will receive a premium of Rs. 6.00. The Lot size of Tata Steel say 5500. Unlike traditional Covered Call strategy of buying 1 lot stock simultaneously, the traders make strategy to buy Tata Steel stocks 1 lot in 4 phases; if the stock price increases. This system of buying stocks in phase manner is synonymous with the dollar cost averaging (roughly 25%). The purchase of stocks in phases depend upon the pace of the stock price movement. On the other hand, if stock price decreases the traders don't do anything. By and by, if stock price bounce back and surpasses the 1st buying price, be ready to buy 2nd phase and so on. Before surpassing the sold call strike price, buy balance stocks to make it complete lot size. The details of phase wise transactions are as follow.

Sl. No.	Stock Price	No. of Stocks Buy	Cumulative Stock	Weighted Average Price
1	120	1500	1500	120.00
2	123	1500	3000	121.50
3	126	1500	4500	123.00
4	130	1000	5500	124.30
Total		5500		124.30

After completion of four phases of buy, the traders could accumulate stocks of Tata Steel equal to one lot, i.e., 5500 Nos. at an average price of Rs. 124.30. In this case, the traders stay with the trade to wait & watch. If stock price further increases, this strategy will give profit. The upside is fully protected. The downside is partly protected, up to the breakeven point. The breakeven point is average stock price minus premium received.

<u>Analysis of profit & loss at various levels:-</u>

For buying stocks at average price of Rs. 124.30/-, you have to pay Rs. 124.30 per share.

For 130 Call option 1 lot sell, premium received = Rs. 6/-

Net debit = 6 – 124.30 = (-) Rs. 118.30/- (Debit)

The overall cash flow of the strategy at different expiry level:

Case 1 – Market expires at 110 (below the average buy price of stock)

    i.   The long stock position will be in loss of Rs. 14.30

    ii. Strike Price 130 sold call will expire worthless & we keep the entire premium of Rs. 6/-.

    iii. Total Loss = - 14.30 + 6 = (-) Rs. 8.30/- multiplied by Lot Size = - 8.30 x 5500 = (-) Rs 45650/-

Case 2 - Market expires at 118.30 (Break Even Point = Stock bought price - Net Credit)

i. The long stock position will be in loss of Rs. = 6/-

ii. Strike Price 130 sold call will expire worthless & we keep the entire premium of Rs. 6/-.

iii. Total Loss = - 6 + 6 = 0; multiplied by Lot Size = 0 x 5500 = Zero.

Case 3 - Market expires at 120 (below the average buy price of stock)

i. The long stock position will be in loss of Rs. 4.30

ii. Strike Price 130 sold call will expire worthless & we keep the entire premium of Rs. 6/-.

iii. Total Profit = 6 – 4.30 = Rs. 1.70 multiplied by Lot Size = 1.70 x 5500 = Rs. 9350/-

Case 4 - Market expires at 124.30 (at the average buy price of stock)

i. The long stock position will be in no loss or profit.

ii. Strike Price 130 sold call will expire worthless & we keep the entire premium of Rs. 6/-.

iii. Total Profit = Rs. 6/- multiplied by Lot Size = 6 x 5500 = Rs. 33,000/-

Case 5 - Market expires at 130 (at the sold price of option)

i. The long stock position will be in profit of Rs. 5.70

ii. Strike Price 130 sold call will expire worthless & we keep the entire premium of Rs. 6/-.

iii. Total Profit = 5.70 + 6.00 = Rs. 11.70 multiplied by Lot Size = 11.70 x 5500 = Rs. 64,350/-

Case 6 - Market expires at 140 (above the sold price of option)

i. The long stock position will be in profit of Rs. = 15.70

ii. Strike Price 130 sold call will be assigned & in loss of Rs. 10/-; The net payoff will be – 10 + 6 = (-) Rs. 4/-.

iii. Total Profit = 15.70 - 4 = Rs. 11.70 multiplied by Lot Size = 11.70 x 5500 = Rs. 64350/-

Case 7 - Market expires at 150 (above the sold price of option)

i. The long stock position will be in profit of Rs. = 25.70

ii. Strike Price 130 sold call will be assigned & in loss of Rs. 20/-; The net payoff will be – 20 + 6 = (-) Rs. 14/-.

iii. Total Profit = 25.70 - 14 = Rs. 11.70 multiplied by Lot Size = 11.70 x 5500 = Rs. 64350/-

The upside is fully protected. However, whatever may be the upside movement, the profit will be capped at the level of strike price of short call.

Summary in Tabular Form:

Sl. No.	Items	Stock Closing Price at Expiry					Remarks
		110	118.30	120	124.30	130	
1	Credit/ Debit received	(- 124.30 + 6) = (–) Rs. 118.30					Debit
2	Payout from Long Stock at 124.30	110	118.30	120	124.30	130	

3	Payout from Short Call SP 130	0	0	0	0	0	
4	Net Payoff	-8.30	0	1.70	6.00	11.70	
5	Profit/ Loss	-456650	0	9350	333000	64350	Lot Size = 5500

In making this strategy of modified Covered Call,

Max Profit = Premium Received + (Strike Price of Short Call – Av. Purchase Price of Underlying) - Commissions

= 6.00 + (130-124.30) = 11.70 x (Lot size of stock i.e., 5500) - Commissions

Max Profit Achieved When Price of Underlying >= Strike Price of Short Call,

i.e., when the stock price is greater than equal to 130.

Maximum Loss = Unlimited

Down side is partly protected; limited to the level equivalent to the premium received by selling the call option. Hence up to (Average Purchase price of stock –

premium received) level, the strategy is protected. i.e., 124.30 – 6.00 = 118.30 level.

Loss Occurs When Price of Underlying < Average Purchase Price of Underlying - Premium Received,

i.e., losses are unlimited when the stock price falls below (124.30 – 6.00 = 118.30) level.

Breakeven Point =Average Purchase Price of Underlying - Premium Received

i.e., 124.30 – 6.00 = 118.30, the level at which no profit, no loss.

If the stock price rebound from the short call strike price and plunges down, the strategy is safe up to the level of average price minus premium received. In this case, the traders or investors are ought to exit the strategy.

During establishment of modified Covered Call strategy, there will be profit if the stock price starts increasing. Maximum profit will be achieved at 130 levels. After crossing 130 levels, no further profit will be gained, rather loss will be incurred exponentially. Above 130 levels, the losses from short call cannot offset by the gain from stock appreciation. Thus, averaging must be done and lot size to be completed before reaching the short call strike price. Once achieved the lot size before reaching short call strike price, there will be no loss with upside movement of stock price. Whatever may be the expiry level above 130, maximum profit will be capped at the level of short call strike price, amounting to Rs. 11.70 x 5500 = 64350/-

When the stock price falls below the breakeven point i.e., 118.30 level, Loss will be occurred and start increasing. Maximum Loss will be unlimited below 118.30 level. Always trade with stop loss.

STOCK REPAIR STRATEGY

Stock Repair Strategy: - After thorough research and screening, the investors buy stocks. Stocks should be bought in phase wise manner with strict stop loss. If stop loss is triggered, get out of the trade. If you are successful and trade is in your favour you can book profit. If you did not use stop loss and the stock price unexpectedly drops, there are 4 alternatives to be considered.

i.   Close out the position for a small loss.

ii.   Investing more in to the position by averaging down, if it is blue chips stocks.

iii.   Holding on to the stock until the prices bounce back with a hope to recover.

iv.   Implementing Stock Repair Strategy.

It is unwise to add more to a loosing position. It is also not desirable to hold on to a loosing stock in the hope of bounce back. Simply get out of the trade with loss booking. In case you failed to square off the position, thinking that the stock could be bounce back in short term or you want to stay some more time in the market and in the meanwhile the stock price declines 10-20%. In such cases, Stock Repair Strategy can be employed if the traders or investors anticipate the stock price to rise moderately in short term. Stock Repair Strategy is meant for repair the break down stock and reduces the Break Even Price without any additional cost & downside risk.

Sell 2 OTM call at SP 130
Buy price of stock at av. price of 125
Buy 1 ATM call at SP 110

You have bought 1 lot of share at an Av. Price of Rs.125. Stock price comes to 110. You buy 1 ATM call at SP 110 & sell 2 OTM Call at SP 130. The strategy costs you nothing as the premium received from selling 2 OTM call option offsets the cost of purchasing one lower strike price ATM call. Thus Stock Repair strategy reduces the Break Even Price (BEP) of the original trade without any additional cost. When selecting Strike Price for the Stock Repair, use the short strike as your target where you expect the stock to move back to.

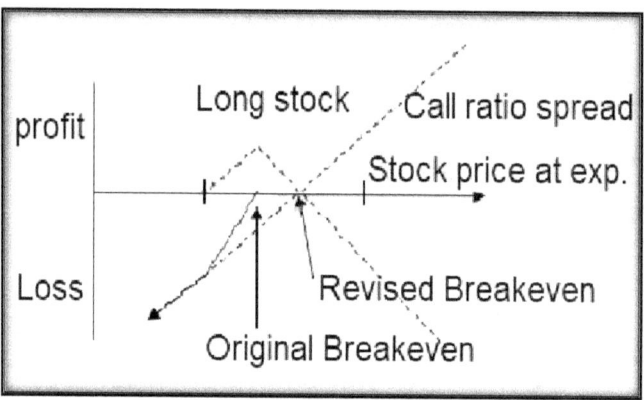

When a strategy stops working or goes beyond expectation, repairing is done to minimize the loss. Repair strategies are an integral part of any trading plan. The traders or investors who have encountered any substantial loss in a position in stock market; either in stock or option trading shall opt to sell/buy and take the loss or hold the position with a hope that the discrepancy shall be reconciled.

Example

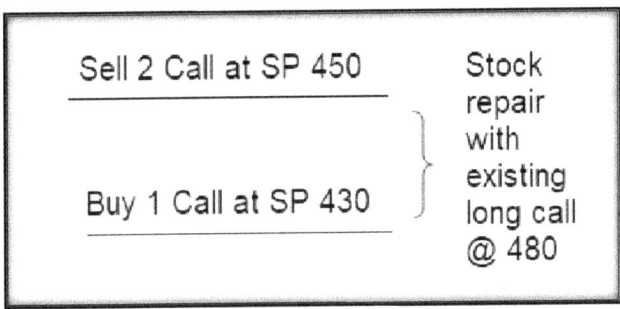

Suppose someone has bought 1 lot share of some F & O stock, say Tata Motors at Rs. 480/- and now the stock is trading at Rs. 440/-. The investor or trader is in loss of Rs. 40/-. Lot size of Tata Motors = 1425. Total loss equals to 40 x 1425 = 57000. If it is felt that, the sentiment of market is mild to moderately bullish and the investors want to initiate a Stock repair strategy against the existing stock. To establish the repair strategy, the investors have to buy 1 Call option at lower strike price (suppose at 430) and sell 2 call options at higher strike price (say 450). By selling two call options at Strike Price of 450, the investor will receive a total premium of (2 x 2) = Rs. 4.00.

By buying one call option at SP 430, the investor have to pay Rs. 5/-.

Net premium = 4 – 5 = - 1

The overall cash flow of the strategy at different expiry level:

Case 1 – Market expires at 430 (at the buy price of Call)

i. The long stock position will be in loss of Rs. - 50/-.

ii. Strike Price 430 buy call will expire worthless & the traders will loose the entire premium of Rs. 5/-.

iii. Strike Price 450 sold call 2 Nos. will expire worthless & the trader will keep the entire premium of Rs. 4/-.

iv. Total Loss = - 50 - 5 + 4 = (-) Rs. 51/- multiplied by Lot Size = - 51 x 1425 = (-) Rs. 72675/-

Case 2 - Market expires at 440 (below the sell price of Call)

    i. The long stock position will be in loss of Rs. = 40/-.

    ii. Strike Price 430 buy call will be in profit of Rs. 10/- & the net payoff = 10 – 5 = Rs. 5/-.

    iii. Strike Price 450 sold call 2 Nos. will expire worthless & the trader will keep the entire premium of Rs. 4/-.

    iv. Total Loss = - 40 + 5 + 4 = (-) Rs. 31/- multiplied by Lot Size = - 31 x 1425 = (-) Rs. 44175/-

Case 3 - Market expires at 450 (at the sold price of Call)

    i. The long stock position will be in loss of Rs. = 30/-.

    ii. Strike Price 430 buy call will be in profit of Rs. 20/- & the net payoff = 10 – 5 = Rs. 5/-.

iii. Strike Price 450 sold call 2 Nos. will expire worthless & the trader will keep the entire premium of Rs. 4/-.

iv. Total Loss = - 30 + 5 + 4 = (-) Rs. 21/- multiplied by Lot Size = - 21 x 1425 = (-) Rs. 29925/-

In this manner, the stock has been repaired to some extent. Stock repair strategy does not involve extra cost and additional down side risk, but increases the probability of recovering from the long established losses. On the other hand, reduces the breakeven. The initial loss of Rs. 57000/- has been reduced to Rs. 29925/-. If the upward movement is anticipated further, Stock repair strategy is established further by buying 1 call at 450 and selling 2 calls at 460.

Selling two call options at Strike Price of 460, the investor will receive a total premium of (2 x 3) = Rs. 6.00. By buying one call option at SP 450, the investor have to pay Rs. 5/-.

Net premium = 6 – 5 = 1

The overall cash flow of the strategy at different expiry level:

Case 1 – Market expires at 450 (at the buy price of Call)

    i. The long stock position will be in loss of Rs. = 30/-.

    ii. Strike Price 450 buy call will expire worthless & the traders will loose the entire premium of Rs. 5/-.

    iii. Strike Price 460 sold call 2 Nos. will expire worthless & the trader will keep the entire premium of Rs. 6/-.

    iv. Total Loss = - 30 - 5 + 6 = (-) Rs. 29/- multiplied by Lot Size = - 29 x 1425 = (-) Rs. 41325/-

Case 2 - Market expires at 460 (at the sold price of Call)

    i. The long stock position will be in loss of Rs. = 20/-.

    ii. Strike Price 450 buy call will be in profit & net payoff = 20 – 5 = Rs. 15/-.

iii. Strike Price 460 sold call 2 Nos. will expire worthless & the trader will keep the entire premium of Rs. 6/-.

iv. Total Loss = - 20 + 15 + 6 = Rs. 1/- multiplied by Lot Size = 1 x 1425 = Rs. 1425/-

Case 3 - Market expires at 470 (above the sold price of Call)

i. The long stock position will be in loss of Rs. = 10/-.

ii. Strike Price 450 buy call will be in profit & net payoff = 20 – 5 = Rs. 15/-.

iii. Strike Price 460 sold call 2 Nos. will be assigned & the trader will be in loss, net payoff = - 10 + 6 = (-) Rs. 4/-.

iv. Total Loss = - 10 + 15 - 4 = Rs. 1/- multiplied by Lot Size = 1 x 1425 = Rs. 1425/-

In this manner, with increase of stock price and implementing stock repair strategy, the loss from the long stock gradually decreases. The initial loss of Rs. 57000/- has been considerably reduced to Rs. 1425/-. This is the power of stock repair strategy. However, if stock price is in down trends, this strategy does not work. Wait for the correction and start repair work, soon the stock price shows positive sentiments and price appreciation.

Selling single option, either Call or Put is considered 'naked' because the position is vulnerable, if move in opposite direction. There is no risk protection if the stock moves against the expectation. In options strategy, the stock price has to move in the direction of expectation. Otherwise, repair strategy is to be adopted.

WEBSITES MAY BE SEEN

google.com

investing.com

tradingview.com

nseindia.com

bseindia.com

moneycontrol.com

rediffmoney.com

icicidirect.com

BOOKS MAY BE READ

1. Intelligent Investor   Benjamin Graham
2. Options made easy   Guy Cohen
3. The Option Trader   George Jabbour
   Hand Book   & Phillip Budwick
4. Getting Started in Options   Michael Thomsett
5. Learn to Earn   Peter Lynch
6. Business Adventure   John Brooks
7. Random Walk Down   Burton G. Malkeil
   Wall Street
8. Rule No. 1   Phil Town
9. Stocks for the Long Run   Jeremy J. Siegel
10. Where are the   Fred Schwed
    Customers' Yachts?
11. How I Made $ 2000000   Nicolas Darvas
    in the Stock Market
12. Trading for a Living   Dr. Alexander Elder
13. Mastering the Trade   John F. Carter
14. Trend Following   Michael Covel

ABOUT THE AUTHOR

Er. Sudhir Kumar Sahu was born to Sj. Sarat Kumar Sahu & Smt. Jagyanseni Sahu on 9th October 1965. Now he is working as Superintending Engineer, Main Dam Division, Burla. Graduated from College of Engineering & Technology, OUAT, Bhubaneswar in 1988 and joined in the department of Water Resources, Govt. of Odisha as Assistant Engineer way back in 1994 and worked in different irrigation projects in different capacity. He has been associated with 14 professional bodies and associations pertaining to engineering organizations. He is also a fellow of the Indian Water Resources Society & Indian Association of Hydrologists.

He has already published ten books namely "The Portfolio of Mythological Events", "The Portfolio of National & International Events", "The Kernel of Stock Market Investing", "The Compilation of Options Strategy" , "The Precept of Stop Loss", "The Paradox of Put Call Ratio", "Iron Condor & Reverse Iron Condor" & "Iron Butterfly & Reverse Iron Butterfly", "Ichimoku Clouds" & "Heiken Ashi Candles" etc. in Amazon.com. This is his 11th book. His better half Smt. Sasmita Sahoo, P.G. Diploma in Nutrition & Dietetics and home makers; having been blessed with two daughters; Samanwita & Samapika. Samanwita Pursued B.Tech. (Comp. Sc.) & working as module lead in LTIMindtree Ltd. and Samapika studying BA in Delhi University, a Civil Service aspirant.

www.ingramcontent.com/pod-product-compliance
Lightning Source LLC
Chambersburg PA
CBHW070612220526
45467CB00003B/1396